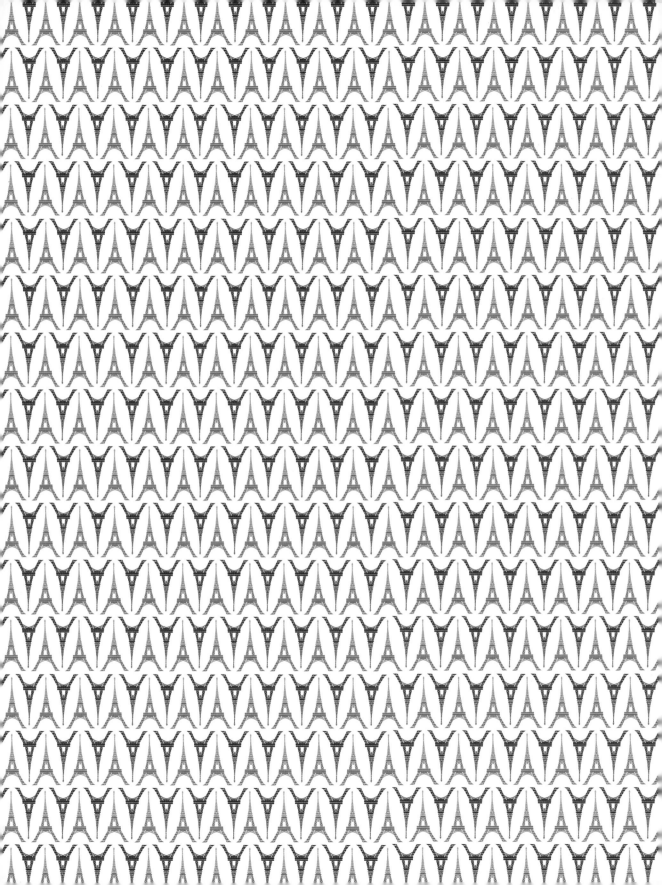

At the Table in

PARIS

AT THE
TABLE
IN
PARIS

Recipes from the
best cafés and bistros

Jan Thorbecke Verlag

MENU
les plats du jour

Upon entering a bistro, say how
many of you there are *(pour deux,
s'il vous plaît)*, and you'll then be
offered a table.

WELCOME TO
PARIS

A map of Paris with its countless sights is temptingly laid out before us. An area of 105 km²/65 miles is packed with a plethora of impressions and ways of life, and everywhere there is something new to be discovered – not least new dishes and aromas.

FINDING YOUR WAY AROUND PARIS

In order to find somewhere in Paris, locals and travel guides usually use two parameters: the arrondissement and the metro station. The arrondissements are 20 urban districts into which the city of Paris inside the inner ring road *Boulevard Périphérique* (where the city wall used to be) is divided. The numbering begins with the 1st arrondissement by the Louvre, after which a clockwise spiral leads to the classic *Rive Gauche* districts 5, 6 and 7 on the left bank of the Seine and the 18th arrondissement, Montmartre, continuing to the 20th, the Belleville district in the northeast. The arrondissement is indicated in every address, as the number forms the end of the postcode. The Louvre's postcode is thus 75001, Montmartre's is 75018 and Belleville's is 75020.

Each arrondissement has its own character, and this also applies to the **GASTRONOMY**. Thus the 13th is home to an abundance of Asian restaurants, the 14th traditionally has a lot of crêperies, and in the 11th you'll find fashionable cafés and bars for night owls, but also confectioners. You can get high-quality meals and indulge in nostalgic repasts in the 2nd and 3rd arrondissements, the 3rd and 4th arrondissements include the old Jewish quarter and offer myriad varieties of Jewish cuisine, while the 18th arrondissement boasts African food.

If you wish to experience Paris on foot you can do so using the signposted routes *Traversée de Paris GRP1* and *GRP2*, which traverse the city from north to south and east to west.
https://www.gr-infos.com/grp-paris.htm

GETTING ABOUT

Tickets are available online:
www.batobus.com

www.ratp.fr/decouvrir/coulisses/
au-quotidien/le-saviez-vous-le-
metro-aerien

www.velib-metropole.fr
An English version of the website
is available:
www.velib-metropole.fr/
en_GB/service

BATOBUS. The *Bateaux Mouches*, which ply the Seine, are world-famous. Less well known is the fact that Paris's public-transport operator runs its own boat-shuttle service, calling at nine stops along the Seine – from the *Jardin de Plantes* in the east of the city to the Eiffel Tower in the west. With a day pass you can come and go as you please.

METRO AÉRIEN (ELEVATED RAILWAY). What form of transport could be any more typical of the city than the Paris Métro? It's highly recommended if you want to get from one point to another easily. If you are planning to travel frequently you should consider a carnet, i.e. a book of ten tickets, now available as the *navigo* chip card, or immediately book a *visite* day or multi-day ticket. Even though many metro stations exude the charm of art nouveau, it's a shame that whilst travelling you see nothing of the city – but city views are also possible: the *Métro aérien* (aerial metro) encircles the city with the lines 2 and 6. Most of the time you travel on elevated tracks and can enjoy the view.

Hire a bike and drop it off elsewhere? **VÉLIB** The metro is of course practical and cheap, but when the weather's nice, cycling through Paris gives you a wonderful feeling of freedom. As recently as 20 years ago you needed to be very courageous or just plain mad to venture into the mêlée of Paris traffic on a bike, but new urban architecture and the establishment of Vélib bike hire have fundamentally changed the city. The blue-and-green rental bikes are to be seen everywhere. There are about 20,000 bikes and 1,400 docking points, where you can hire bikes or drop them off, including as a tourist. The best option is to download the app at home and search for Vélib Paris on YouTube. You'll then get an explanation of how to collect bikes from the docking points and what to bear in mind (just a note, don't borrow a bike that's damaged!).

BREAKFAST

13

Baguette
'Magique'

This baguette has earned the epithet 'magique' because the recipe is so simple and you don't need a food processor, as there's no kneading involved. It tastes like a proper baguette from a French bistro – crispy on the outside and soft and fluffy on the inside.

FOR 3 BAGUETTES

10 g (½ oz) yeast
1 pinch of sugar
300 ml (10 fl oz/1¼ cups) water
380 g (13½ oz) flour (type 550)
plus extra for dusting
1½ tsp salt

❶ Dissolve the yeast and sugar in the water, then add the flour and salt and mix briefly with a wooden spoon until combined to form a dough.
❷ Cover the dough, ideally with foil or a cloth, and let it rise for 2 hours at room temperature.
❸ Generously spread flour over the work surface and carefully put the almost-liquid dough on it, making sure not to deflate the dough.
❹ Sprinkle flour on the dough, divide it into three equal-sized pieces using a dough scraper, and very carefully transfer the pieces to an oblong baguette tray. Then place on a metal sheet – preferably a baguette sheet.
❺ Bake the baguettes for 20 minutes in an oven preheated to 240°C fan (500°F, with circulating air). During the baking process place a small bowl with plenty of water on the bottom of the oven.
❻ Allow the baguettes to cool.

BRIOCHE

PARISIENNE

or Brioche à Tête

❶ Mix the yeast and sugar with the lukewarm milk, then stir in the flour, 1 egg and vanilla. Add the butter and knead in to form a dough. Cover and leave it to rise for 40 minutes somewhere warm.

❷ Thoroughly grease the brioche moulds.

❸ Once again knead the brioche dough, then divide into 12 pieces. Shape the brioche dough into rounds (you can opt for the traditional double sphere shape if you prefer), then place into the moulds.

❹ Place the rounds on a tray and let rest, uncovered, for 30 minutes.

❺ Preheat the oven to 180°C/190°C fan (400°F).

❻ Whisk the egg with the milk and brush the brioches with the mixture, before baking them for 25 to 30 minutes in the oven. During the baking process place a bowl of hot water on the bottom of the oven.

12

FOR APPROX. 12 BRIOCHES
1 cube of fresh yeast
60 g (2 oz) sugar
250 ml (8 fl oz) lukewarm milk
500 g (1 lb 2 oz) flour
2 eggs
¼ tsp vanilla paste
60 g (2 oz) butter, cut into
small pieces

To glaze
1 egg
2 tbsp milk

Croissants
au Beurre

Soft on the inside and nice and crispy on the outside – you'll actually only find classic croissants in France, but using this recipe you can now also have them for breakfast at home!

16

FOR APPROX. 16 CROISSANTS
15 g (½ oz) yeast
2 tbsp lukewarm water
300 g (1 lb 2 oz) flour
50 g (1¾ oz) sugar
10 g (½ oz) salt
280 ml (6 fl oz/¾ cup) milk
180 g (6½ oz) soft butter
1 egg, for brushing

TOP TIP
You can also prebake and freeze the dough. Store them well sealed the night before baking, then in the morning briefly finish baking them in the oven, and they'll taste nearly as good as freshly baked ones!

❶ To make the puff pastry, stir the yeast into the lukewarm water. In a large bowl, blend the flour, sugar and salt. Gradually add the (not too cold) milk, and finally stir in the yeast mixture. Then knead the dough for at least 15 minutes. Shape into a ball, cover and let it rest for 2 hours.

❷ After the dough has rested, roll it out into a rectangle. Remove any flour residue from the dough. The butter should be about as soft as the dough. Spread the soft butter from the middle to the edge (leaving a 2 cm (¾ in) edge). Now fold the corners in towards the middle.

❸ Once again roll the dough out into a rectangle, and again fold in towards the middle. Repeat this process several times (approx. 7 to 8). Between each folding allow the dough to rest.

❹ Then roll out and cut into 16 triangles. Roll the long side towards the tip, and bend the roll to form a crescent shape. The tip should be in the middle. Again let the croissants rest for 2 hours.

❺ Preheat the oven to 240°C fan (500°F).

❻ Whisk 1 egg in a small bowl and brush the croissants with it.

❼ First bake the croissants for 5 minutes at 240°C, then for a further 10 to 15 minutes at 170°C fan (375°F).

❽ Remove the croissants from the oven as soon as they're golden brown.

Pains au Chocolat

Chocolate Croissants

Pains au chocolat are rectangular – not crescent-shaped like croissants. Perfect pains au chocolat need a little practise, but the taste of these warm, flaky chocolatey pastries, fresh out of the oven, is next to nothing.

❶ Follow the recipe for the croissant dough on page 18 up to the rolling out of the dough.
❷ Cut the chocolate into strips, to create small chocolate sticks (about 1.5 × 1.5 × 8 cm/½ in × ½ in × 3¼ in).
❸ Preheat the oven to 180°C fan/400°F.
❹ Now cut the dough into rectangles the same length as the chocolate sticks. Place a chocolate stick on a rectangle and roll it in, then put a second chocolate stick on it and roll it again, so there are 2 chocolate sticks in each pain au chocolat. Then cut off the dough.
❺ Lay the individual pains au chocolat on a baking sheet, leaving enough space between them for rising, and brush with the beaten egg. Allow to rise again.
❻ Bake in the oven for approx. 15 minutes, or until golden brown.

16

FOR APPROX. 16 PAINS AU CHOCOLAT
dough recipe for croissants – p.18
300 g (10½ oz) dark chocolate
1 egg, beaten, for brushing

GRANOLA

with nuts and a hint of cinnamon & vanilla

2

FOR 2 PEOPLE

150 g (5½ oz/1½ cups) rolled oats
50 g (1¾ oz/½ cup) flaked almonds
50 g (1¾ oz/½ cup) hazelnuts
or walnuts
1 pinch of cinnamon
¼ tsp vanilla extract
1 pinch of salt
50 g (1¾ oz) coconut oil
65 g (2¼ oz) honey

PREPARATION

❶ Preheat the oven to 180°C fan (350°F).
❷ Combine the rolled oats, nuts, cinnamon, vanilla and salt in a large bowl.
❸ Melt the coconut oil in a saucepan and stir in the honey, to melt, and the nut mixture.
❹ Spread the combined ingredients on a baking sheet lined with parchment paper.
❺ Bake for 20 minutes, turning the granola over now and again using a spatula.
❻ Remove the granola from the oven and allow to cool completely. Break up into pieces and store in an airtight container.

TOP TIP
Perfect for breakfast with yoghurt
and fresh fruit.

Pain Perdu
or: *French Eggy Bread*

2

FOR 2 PEOPLE

500 ml (17 fl oz/generous 2 cups)
milk
100 g (3½ oz) sugar
½ sachet (4 g) of vanilla sugar
2 eggs
pinch of salt
2 slices white bread
2 tbsp oil or 1 tbsp butter

PREPARATION

❶ Put the milk and sugars in a bowl and combine.
In a second bowl whisk the eggs and salt.
❷ Dip both sides of the bread slices in the milk
and sugar mixture, so they become saturated.
❸ Now briefly turn the soaked slices of bread
in the second bowl containing the eggs.
❹ Heat a little oil or butter in a pan and fry the
slices until they're crispy and golden brown.

SHOPPING
FOR GOURMETS

KITCHEN APPLIANCES: DEHILLERIN

Dehillerin is a kitchen shop like something from the good old days. It has a wonderfully old-fashioned atmosphere, and here in the middle of Paris, chefs will find everything they might wish for: copper kettles, cookie cutters, oyster knives, other knives for scallops ... plus expert advice. Both a treasure trove and a journey through time.

SPICES: G. DETOU

What would French cuisine be, and what would Paris bistros be, without the diversity of their spices? A large proportion of them, partly in catering packs for the restaurant trade, are to be found at G. Detou, where the spice containers are stacked right up to the ceiling. And lovers of cake decoration will find just what they want here.

SWEETS: À LA MÈRE DE FAMILLE

A la Mère de Famille is a sweet shop like one from your grandmother's time, with big jars full of brightly coloured sweets, and beautifully presented candied fruits and pralines. Although the business now has branches in many parts of the city, you really should visit the historic shop in the 9th arrondissement, which is in fact under a preservation order. It's scarcely changed since the 19th century, and is enchanting, with its chandeliers, étagères, wooden drawers and displays from the time of its foundation.

DEYROLLE

Deyrolle is more than a shop – almost a small museum. On the first floor, over the ground-floor bookshop, is the natural-history gallery, with its stuffed animals, minerals, shells etc. For years Deyrolle produced display boards for school classrooms on topics such as 'trees' and 'orchids', as well as subjects such as 'jam', 'coffee' and 'bread'. The most beautiful of these nostalgic boards are now on sale as reprints.

OPEN-AIR SHOPPING: MARKETS

Parisians like shopping at markets, and the city boasts many weekly markets and covered markets. Things are particularly lively, colourful and diverse in and around Beauvau covered market on the Place d'Aligre. In this market you can marvel at an unbelievable array of cheeses, but they sell geese and whole calf's heads, too. In the square in front of the market there's also a vibrant and unusual flea market, selling books, second-hand clothes and craftwork. Around the square are bars and wine bars, in front of which people stand watching the comings and goings, glass in hand.

SHOPPING IN THE RAIN: THE ARCADES

What can you do in Paris when it's raining? There are the museums, of course, but those of you of a more consumerist bent might prefer to explore the old shopping arcades, which exude 19th-century charm.

With its little street maps the French website *passagesetgaleries.fr* presents a variety of walks *(itinéraires)*, which will take you through the highly atmospheric Paris of the 19th century, mostly under cover, e.g. Galerie Véro-Dodat, Galerie Colbert, Galerie Vivienne, Passage Choiseul, Passage du Marché St Honoré and Galerie de la Madeleine. These locations are in the 1st and 2nd arrondissements.

CULINARY GIFTS

If you're unable to transport wine, champagne or cheese, you might try resorting to mustard: **LA BOUTIQUE MAILLE**, 6 Place de la Madeleine, 8 Arrondissement

Fine tea from France is even easier to transport: **BOUTIQUE MARIAGE FRÈRES**, 32 Rue du Bourg-Tibourg, 4 Arrondissement
DAMMANN FRÈRES, 15 Place des Vosges, 4 Arrondissement; 101bis, Rue Mouffetard, 5 Arrondissement; 145 Boulevard Saint-Germain, 6 Arrondissement *(and others)*

The art of macaron-making at its finest: **LADURÉE**, 14 Rue de Bretagne, 3 Arrondissement; 21 Rue Bonaparte, 6 Arrondissement; in the store Printemps, 62 Boulevard Haussmann, 9 Arrondissement *(and others)*

By Way Of
A SNACK

CROQUE
MONSIEUR

**This truly French goodie is *the* bistro classic: a baked sandwich
with béchamel sauce, cheese and ham**

FOR 2 PEOPLE

25 g (¾ oz) butter
25 g (¾ oz) flour
125 ml (4 fl oz/½ cup) milk
salt & pepper
grated nutmeg
4 slices of white bread
butter for brushing and frying
2 slices of cooked ham
75 g (2½ oz) grated Gruyère
or Comté

PREPARATION

❶ For the béchamel sauce, melt the butter in a saucepan over low heat. Gradually add the flour and stir it in. Then slowly pour in the milk, and stir until a creamy consistency is achieved. Finally, season the sauce with salt, pepper and nutmeg, and put to one side.
❷ Preheat the oven to 180°C fan/190°C (400°F).
❸ Brush 4 slices of white bread with butter. Place two of them buttered side down, and spread them with two-thirds of the béchamel sauce. Layer on a slice of ham, followed by a handful of grated cheese, and finally the remaining béchamel sauce. Lay a slice of white bread on top, buttered side up.
❹ Now bake the croques in the oven for about 20 minutes (or use a sandwich machine), until golden brown.

TOP TIP
Instead of slices of white bread you can also use slices of brioche (page 17) – as is very popular in many regions of France.

CROQUE *Madame*

A dish as popular as the croque is of course modified time and again in every family and in every kitchen. According to the French Wikipedia a **CROQUE-MADAME** is simply a **CROQUE MONSIEUR** with a fried egg on top, but we're taking the croque madame as a basis for another version of the croque: without béchamel sauce, no cooking in the oven, and thus quicker to make.

FOR 2 PEOPLE

4 slices of white bread
30 g (1 oz) grated cheese (Gruyère or Emmental)
2 slices of cooked ham
10 g (½ oz) butter
2 eggs
salt & pepper

PREPARATION

❶ Sprinkle the grated cheese on the slices of bread, season with the salt and pepper, then lay the ham on top. Top with the remaining two slices of bread.

❷ Melt the butter in a pan, but don't let it brown. Crack the eggs into the pan and fry them. Remove and put to one side.

❸ In the same pan, lightly brown the two croques on both sides. Place on a plate and garnish each of them with the fried egg.

Galettes au Sarrasin

Breton Bulgur Crêpes

This speciality from Brittany is also widely available in Paris, e.g. in bistros as a snack, or freshly prepared, to be eaten with your hands. It can be topped and filled with anything you wish – be it sweet or savoury, vegetarian or with meat. Here, we have given two options, with spring onion and egg or ham and cheese – take your pick.

2

FOR 2 PEOPLE

150 g (5½ oz) bulgur flour
3 eggs
pinch of salt
220 ml (7½ fl oz/scant cup) water
butter, for frying
salt & pepper

Cheese and ham version
50 g (1¾ oz) grated Gruyère
2 slices cooked ham

Spring onion version
1 spring onion

PREPARATION

❶ Whisk the flour, one egg and salt in a large bowl. Gradually stir in the water to make a smooth batter.
❷ Let the batter rest for at least 1 hour.
❸ Heat the butter in a pan and fry wafer-thin galettes until golden on each side. Remove to a tray and keep warm in a low oven.
❹ Before serving, lay each galette in a hot pan again and place your chosen filling of cheese and ham or egg with spring onions sprinkled on top. Season with salt and pepper.
❺ Fold the sides of the galette in, and carefully slide onto a plate to serve.

TARTE *flambée*

Alsatian Bacon and Onion Tart

2

FOR 2 PEOPLE

150 g (5½ oz) flour (type 550), plus
extra for dusting

1 tsp salt

100 ml (3½ fl oz) water

125 g (4½ oz) back bacon or
streaky bacon

1 onion

4–5 tbsp crème fraîche

pepper and a little grated nutmeg

PREPARATION

❶ For the dough, mix the flour with the salt and water, but without kneading – just combine the ingredients to form a dough. Let it rest for 30 minutes.

❷ Meanwhile, cut the onion into thin slices and dice the bacon.

❸ Preheat the oven to 190°F fan (400°F) and line a baking sheet with parchment paper.

❹ Roll out the dough on a dusted work surface until thin. Carefully transfer to the baking sheet.

❺ Spread the crème fraîche on the dough. Distribute the onion rings and diced bacon evenly on top.

❻ Season with pepper and nutmeg.

❼ Bake for about 20 minutes.

Omelette
NATURE

No, this isn't an ordinary omelette!
A real French omelette is simple, with a hint of butter.

PREPARATION

❶ Whisk the eggs in a bowl, but don't let them foam too much. Season with salt and pepper.
❷ Melt the butter in a large pan over a high heat.
❸ Pour the eggs into the pan, making sure they spread out evenly. Reduce the temperature to medium. Let the *omelette nature* slowly set.
❹ When the omelette has almost completely set but is still visibly soft, carefully fold it in half and slide it onto a plate.

FOR 2 PEOPLE

4 eggs
10 g (½ oz) butter
salt & pepper

TOP TIP
Particularly good partners for a classic *omelette nature* are fried mushrooms, fresh smoked salmon or a seasonal tomato salad.

QUICHE

with sun-dried tomatoes and feta

The original form of quiche is the *quiche Lorraine*.
It comes the Lorraine region of France, and the word 'quiche' derives
from the German word 'Kuchen', meaning cake.

12

FOR 1 QUICHE APPROX. 25 CM (10 IN)

200 g (7 oz/1⅔ cups) flour
120 g (4½ oz) butter
3 eggs
200 ml (7 fl oz/scant 1 cup) crème fraîche
100 g (3½ oz) sun-dried cherry tomatoes
100 g (3½ oz) baby spinach
100 g (3½ oz) feta
salt & pepper

PREPARATION

❶ To make the pastry, put the flour, butter and salt into a bowl and knead to form a dough. Then shape the dough into a ball and let it sit for approx. 30 minutes.

❷ Preheat the oven to 180°C fan (400°F) and grease a quiche tin.

❸ Roll the dough out evenly and lay it in the greased quiche tin. Using a fork, carefully prick the base of the dough.

❹ Line the dough base with parchment paper and weigh it down with dried peas or lentils.

❺ Blind-bake for 10 minutes.

❻ Whisk together the eggs and crème fraîche, and season with salt and pepper. Cut the dried tomatoes up finely and dice the feta, then add to the egg–crème fraîche mixture together with the baby spinach.

❼ Remove the blind-baked dough from the oven, take out the parchment paper and dried peas or lentils, and carefully pour the mixture into the pastry shell.

❽ Return the quiche to the oven and bake for a further 30 minutes or until cooked.

TOP TIP

There are many different kinds of quiche. In the Paris bistros quiches are often served with a small mixed salad on the side.

Salade Œuf Poché
with Lardons

Pierce the poached egg on the top of the salad and watch the warm egg yolk drip into the salad – it's an Amélie moment!

FOR 2 PEOPLE

2 eggs
3 tbsp white vinegar
100 g (3½ oz) bacon
4 tbsp olive oil
2 tbsp white wine vinegar
1 tsp mustard
½ tsp agave syrup
½ head of lettuce
salt & pepper

PREPARATION

❶ First poach the eggs. In a large saucepan, bring to a simmer 2 litres (68 fl oz/8½ cups) water and add the white vinegar. Slowly – ideally using a ladle into which the eggs have previously been cracked – slide the eggs in and poach for 3 minutes. Carefully lift out of the water with a ladle and drain on a plate lined with kitchen towel.

❷ Fry the bacon in a hot pan without any oil for about 5 minutes. Remove to a plate lined with kitchen towel to drain off excess oil.

❸ For the dressing, mix the olive oil, white wine vinegar, mustard, agave syrup, and salt and pepper in a small bowl.

❹ Wash the lettuce leaves, separating the leaves and placing them in serving bowls. Toss through the dressing.

❺ Finally scatter the bacon over the lettuce and place a poached egg on top of each portion.

Salade
DE CHÈVRE CHAUD

Lettuce with grilled goat's cheese

In France this salad is served in nearly every bistro. It's quick, and is a perfect summer snack that's also popular as a starter.

2

FOR 2 PEOPLE

2–3 handfuls of salad leaves
1 egg
100 g (3½ oz/1 cup) breadcrumbs
150 g (5½ oz) goat's-cheese log
½ baguette
3 tbsp olive oil
1 tbsp white wine vinegar
1 tsp Dijon mustard
salt & pepper

PREPARATION

❶ Lay the salad leaves on serving plates. Preheat the oven to 160° fan/350°F.
❷ Crack the egg into a bowl and whisk. Sprinkle the breadcrumbs onto a plate.
❸ Cut the goat's cheese into slices 1.5 cm (½ in) thick. Turn the slices of goat's cheese first in the whisked egg, then in the breadcrumbs.
❹ Likewise cut the baguette into slices 1.5 cm thick and top with the goat's cheese slices. Place them on a baking tray lined with parchment paper.
❺ Bake for approx. 5 to 8 minutes.
❻ Meanwhile, prepare the vinaigrette by mixing the olive oil, white wine vinegar, Dijon mustard and salt and pepper.
❼ Top the salad leaves with the goat's-cheese baguette slices, then drizzle with the vinaigrette.

SALADE
Auvergnate

Inspired by the celebrated French chef Alain Ducasse, this Auvergne salad is also fine without the customary boiled potatoes. It's a light summer snack option, and is rounded off by the special use of blue cheese.

PREPARATION

❶ Arrange the salad leaves on serving plates.
❷ Dice the bacon and fry in a pan for 5 minutes until crispy, then drain on a plate lined with kitchen towel.
❸ For the dressing, mix the olive oil, vinegar, mustard and agave syrup, and season with the salt and pepper. Cut the cheese into chunks and coarsely chop the walnuts.
❹ Pour the dressing over the leaves and toss.
❺ Top with the cheese, bacon and walnuts and serve.

FOR 2 PEOPLE

2 to 3 handfuls of colourful mixed
salad leaves
6 slices of bacon
2 tbsp olive oil
1 tbsp white wine vinegar
½ tsp Dijon mustard
½ tsp agave syrup
100 g (3½ oz) blue cheese
or Comté
30 g (1 oz) walnuts
salt & pepper

SALADE
Niçoise

As the name indicates, the Salade Niçoise hails from the region around Nice, but this classic dish is a favourite of the Paris bistros, where it's to be found on nearly every menu. A number of sources even claim it originates from Paris.

2

FOR 2 PEOPLE

100 g (3½ oz) green beans
1 egg
2 tbsp olive oil
1 tbsp white wine vinegar
½ tsp mustard
½ tsp agave syrup
salt & pepper
150 g (5½ oz) mixed salad leaves
½ red onion
2 tomatoes
200 g (7 oz) tinned tuna in olive oil,
drained
2 tbsp pitted black olives

PREPARATION

❶   Blanch the green beans in a saucepan of boiling water for approx. 8 minutes, then rinse under cold running water.

❷   Cook the egg in a saucepan of boiling water for approx. 8 to 10 minutes. Allow to cool, then peel and cut the egg into four segments.

❸   For the dressing, mix the olive oil, white-wine vinegar, mustard, agave syrup, salt and pepper in a jar.

❹   Wash the lettuce, cut into small pieces and divide the salad leaves equally between two dishes. Cut the onion into rings and the tomatoes into eight segments.

❺   Now arrange the onion rings, tomato segments, beans, olives, tuna and hard-boiled egg on the lettuce.

❻   Finally drizzle the dressing over the salad, and ideally serve with slices of baguette.

A CRAVING
FOR GREENERY

PARKS If you're tired of roads and pavements you can sample Paris's many parks. With a bit of luck you'll be able to use one of the heavy iron garden chairs provided for visitors in nearly all the parks. The ones with the comfy backrests are particularly sought after! The Tuileries Garden, between the Louvre and the Champs-Elysées, is world-famous, likewise the Luxembourg Garden on the other side of the Seine. Like most of the numerous parks – and the cemeteries – they're fenced, and are closed in the evening, and the opening hours depend on the season. But there's evening opening at the **CHAMPS DE MARS** below the Eiffel Tower and the **ESPLANADE DES INVALIDES**, for example, as well as in parts of **LA VILLETTE** – a big park in the north of the city. Finding green spots in Paris isn't that hard, but it's worth seeking out these special places. The **PALAIS ROYAL GARDENS** are right in the city centre, but being surrounded by buildings they're easy to miss, and are only accessible via small passages. Their location makes the gardens a calm oasis in the middle of the city, surrounded by historic buildings and with colonnaded arcades around the perimeter.

The **PROMENADE PLANTÉE** or **COULÉE VERTE** is hidden in a completely different way. This park is high up on a former railway embankment / brick viaduct, and is thus on the one hand removed from the hectic street life but on the other hand close to the windows and balconies of the surrounding apartments. The park is just metres wide, but like the old railway it extends 4.5 km/ 2.8 miles from the Bastille far into the east of the city (metro stop Daumesnil).

MESSING AROUND BY THE WATERSIDE by the **CANAL SAINT-MARTIN**, with its picturesque old iron bridges, you're surrounded by trees. The many chic shops and bars in the environs mean you're rarely on your own here. If you follow the canal out of the city it first flows into the big artificial lake **BASSIN DE LA VILLETTE** (with an open-air pool), you will arrive at the **PARC DE LA VILLETTE** – a large green area accommodating numerous smaller gardens that are open to the public, as well as cafés, museums and concert halls.

Wandering along the Seine is not easy because there are high stone walls used as flood barriers

for the city. Down by the water, large sections are taken up by big roads. But things are different in summer. From the beginning of July to the end of August the roads are closed to cars, and are used for cafés, food trucks, deckchairs and children's play areas. The name **PARIS PLAGE** (Paris Beach) derives from the time when truckloads of sand were deposited here on the banks of the Seine. Right by the Seine, a stone's throw from the Jardin de Plantes, is a small sculpture park: the **TINO ROSSI GARDEN**. It's a special place, as you're not separated from the water by high stone walls, but perhaps more so because in fine weather people meet **TO DANCE** on its small platforms. Salsa, tango and rock'n'roll are often just a few metres apart. This park isn't fenced, and it stays open overnight. (Metro stations Jussieu or Austerlitz.)

PICNICS You can stock up for a picnic in the park at one of the little supermarkets or *superettes*, where many Parisians also buy pre-packaged salads, fruit etc. for their lunch. And at the baker's you can of course get baguettes (the slim *flûtes* and even slimmer *ficelles*, both of which are practical for al fresco eating) and lovely little tartlets – plus, with a bit of luck, quiches and tourtes. If you're looking for hearty specialities like this you should make use of *traiteurs*, who sell quiches, pâtés and salads. They often prefer to do catering, but many of them also offer shop sales. Everything under the name of rillette or terrine will be a cross between liver sausage and *foie gras*, and will be great for spreading on bread.

WATER

For picnicking in the park you don't need to schlep a big bottle of water around, because the city is graced by around 30 attractive water fountains, donated by the patron Richard Wallace. For these Wallace fountains you just need a small bottle or a mug, to hold under the stream of water. More recent parks, e.g. the Coulée Verte, often offer drinking water from simpler fountains.

EVENING MEAL
Entrée

59

Bouillabaisse

FISH SOUP WITH ROUILLE

This is a somewhat simplified version of the French classic. The rouille can be made in advance.

4–6

FOR 4 TO 6 PEOPLE

350 g (12 oz) cod fillet
50 ml (1¾ fl oz/3½ tbsp) olive oil,
plus extra
2 pinches saffron
2 onions, finely chopped
2 garlic cloves, finely chopped
1 whole gutted sea bream, scaled
1 sea bass, scaled
200 g (7 oz) mussels
200 g (7 oz) raw shell-on prawns
(shrimp)
1 stick of celery
6 tomatoes, peeled
300 g (10½ oz) potatoes, peeled
1 splash of white wine
1 fennel bulb
grated zest of ½ lemon
1 bay leaf
3 thyme sprigs
1 litre (34 fl oz/4¼ cups) fish stock
salt & pepper

TO SERVE
1 baguette
200 g (7 oz) grated cheese

TOP TIP
The accompanying rouille is a kind
of hot mayonnaise. If you don't
want to make it yourself, it's also
available ready to serve in
well-stocked supermarkets.

❶ The night before making the soup, marinate the cod fillet in 50 ml (1¾ fl oz/3½ tbsp) olive oil, saffron, 1 onion, 1 garlic clove and salt.
❷ The following day clean the sea bream and sea bass, and cut into pieces (leaving the head, tail and skin on), then thoroughly clean the mussels and prawns.
❸ Sauté the remaining onion and garlic in a saucepan together with a splash of olive oil.
❹ Cut the celery, tomatoes and potatoes into cubes, add, and likewise sauté. Add a splash of white wine.
❺ Cut the fennel into small pieces. Add the fish pieces, mussels, prawns (shrimp), lemon zest, remaining pinch of saffron, bay leaf, thyme and fennel to the sautéed vegetables and pour in the stock. Season with salt and pepper and simmer for 30 minutes.
❻ Remove the fish, mussels, prawns and herbs. Prepare the fish pieces for serving by removing the head, tail, skin and bones. Put the fish pieces, mussels and peeled prawns (shrimp) to one side and keep warm until ready to serve.
❼ To give the soup a finer consistency you can now purée the liquid, then strain it.
❽ Briefly sear the marinated cod fillets. Pour the soup into bowls and garnish with the fried and filleted fish, mussels and prawns (shrimp). Serve with rouille on top.

ROUILLE

1 EGG YOLK / 1 GARLIC CLOVE /
1–2 PINCHES SAFFRON /
125 ML (4 FL OZ/½ CUP) RAPESEED OIL / PEPPER /
FLAKED SEA SALT

Put the egg yolk into a small bowl. Crush the garlic and add, together with the saffron, pepper and a pinch of salt. ● Now very slowly add the rapeseed oil, drop by drop, using a whisk, until a creamy consistency is achieved. Season to taste.
● Spread the rouille on grilled or toasted baguette, sprinkle a little grated cheese on it and serve with the bouillabaisse.

Magrets de Canard au Miel

with celeriac purée

2

FOR 2 PEOPLE

INGREDIENTS

2 duck-breast fillets
olive oil
1 tbsp butter
3 tbsp honey
2 tbsp balsamic vinegar
salt & pepper

FOR THE CELERIAC PURÉE

½ celeriac root
200 g (7 oz) waxy potatoes
1 bay leaf
50 ml (1¾ fl oz/3½ tbsp) milk
or cream
2 tbsp butter
grated nutmeg
salt

PREPARATION

❶ Pat the duck breast dry, and use a sharp knife to carefully score the skin and the layer of subcutaneous fat so as to create a criss-cross pattern. Don't cut into the meat. Rub salt into the duck fillet.

❷ Preheat the oven to 180°C fan/400°F.

❸ For the celeriac purée, peel and dice the celeriac and potatoes. Put into a saucepan of water and boil for 20 minutes with the bay leaf and salt. Then strain, remove the bay leaf and replace the lid on the pan to keep the vegetables warm.

❹ In a hot pan, sear the duck breast in a little oil, skin-side down. When the skin side is crispy turn the duck breast over and briefly brown the other side. Remove the pan from the heat.

❺ Spread ½ tablespoon honey on the skin side of each duck fillet, wrap in foil and finish cooking them in the oven for about 8 minutes. (If using a meat thermometer the target core temperature should be approx. 60°C.)

❻ Meanwhile, prepare the honey sauce. Melt the butter in the pan already used for the duck. Then add the remaining honey. Caramelise the honey, stirring constantly, then add the vinegar. Season with a little salt and pepper.

❼ Remove the duck from the oven, let it rest for approx. 5 minutes, then cut into slices and serve with the honey sauce.

❽ For the celeriac purée, heat the milk or cream in a small saucepan, add to the celeriac and potatoes, then mash to form a smooth purée. Stir in the butter, and season with nutmeg and salt.

TAPENADE

with olives

FOR 2 PEOPLE

2 cloves of garlic
400 g (14 oz) pitted black olives
2 tbsp olive oil
salt & pepper
1 baguette

PREPARATION

❶ Peel the garlic cloves and coarsely chop them.
❷ Put the olives in a deep bowl together with the garlic and olive oil, and mix using a hand blender until a fine consistency is achieved (this can also be done in a food processor).
❸ Season with salt and pepper.
❹ Cut the baguette into slices and spread with tapenade.

with anchovies

FOR 2 PEOPLE

2 cloves of garlic
100 g (3½ oz) anchovies
200 g (7 oz) pitted black olives
100 g (3½ oz) capers
2 tbsp olive oil
salt & pepper

PREPARATION

❶ Peel the garlic cloves and coarsely chop them. Likewise, coarsely cut the anchovies.
❷ Put the olives in a deep bowl together with the garlic, anchovies, capers and olive oil, and mix using a hand blender until a fine consistency is achieved (this can also be done in a food processor).
❸ Season with salt and pepper.
❹ Cut the baguette into slices and spread with tapenade.

TOP TIP

The tapenade can be kept in the fridge for several days.

Soufflé AU FROMAGE

2

FOR 2 PEOPLE
30 g (1 oz) butter
30 g (1 oz/¼ cup) flour
250 ml (8 fl oz/1 cup) milk.
2 eggs
100 g (3½ oz) grated Gruyère
grated nutmeg
salt & pepper

PREPARATION

❶   Preheat the oven to 220°C fan (475°F).
❷   For the béchamel sauce, melt the butter in a saucepan over a low heat. Gradually add the flour and stir, to create a homogeneous mixture.
❸   Remove the pan from the heat. Gradually stir in the milk.
❹   Then put the pan back on the stove, and stir the mixture over a low heat until thickened and creamy.
❺   Season the béchamel sauce with nutmeg and salt and pepper, then transfer to a large bowl.
❻   Separate the eggs. Add the yolks to the béchamel sauce one by one, and stir until smooth. Then add the Gruyère and fold in.
❼   Beat the egg whites until stiff, and carefully fold into the béchamel.
❽   Pour the mixture into a greased dish or 2 small soufflé dishes. The dish(es) must not be over two-thirds full, as the soufflé will rise. Bake for approx. 18 to 20 minutes, until well risen and golden yellow on top. (Don't open the oven door during baking.)
❾   The soufflé should be served hot, otherwise it will collapse.

SOUPE À L'OIGNON
FRENCH ONION SOUP

PREPARATION

❶ Slice the onions into rings and finely dice the garlic.

❷ Heat the butter in a saucepan and sauté the onions and garlic. Sprinkle over the flour and cook for another couple of minutes.

❸ Pour in the stock and white wine, stirring well to deglaze the pan, and simmer for approx. 30 minutes over a low heat.

❹ Season with salt and pepper.

❺ Fry the baguette slices until golden in the pan.

❻ Pour the soup into ovenproof soup bowls or terrines, top with the baguette slices and sprinkle with cheese.

❼ Preheat the oven to 230°C (475°F) grill (broil) setting. Place the bowls into the oven and grill (broil) until the cheese is melted and golden brown.

FOR 4 PEOPLE

500 g (1 lb 2 oz) onions
2 cloves of garlic
40 g (1½ oz) butter
20 g (¾ oz) flour
1 litre (34 fl oz/4¼ cups) meat
or vegetable stock
250 ml (8 fl oz/1 cup) white wine
salt & pepper
½ baguette, sliced
100 g (3½ oz) grated mature
aged cheese

S'TEAK TARTARE

with capers and spring onions

2

FOR 2 PEOPLE

2 spring onions (scallions)
½ bunch of chives
2 egg yolks, plus 2 extra egg yolks
to serve (optional)
1 tsp mustard
1 tbsp olive oil
300 g (10½ oz) minced (ground)
beef
1 tbsp capers
1 tbsp Worcestershire sauce
salt & pepper

PREPARATION

❶ Finely chop the spring onions (scallions) and chives.
❷ Put the egg yolks and mustard into a large bowl. Gradually add the olive oil and keep stirring, to form a creamy sauce (like a mayonnaise).
❸ Add the minced (ground) beef, chopped spring onions (scallions), chives, capers and Worcestershire sauce, and combine.
❹ Serve with an egg yolk on top if you like.

TOP TIP

Make sure the ingredients you buy are fresh, especially the mince and the eggs.

The dish should always be served immediately.

TARTARE
de Saumon

with Cognac

FOR 2 PEOPLE

300 g (10½ oz) salmon fillet
(see Tip)
½ bunch of parsley
1 onion
1 egg yolk
1 tbsp cognac
salt & pepper

PREPARATION

❶ Pat the salmon dry and cut into small cubes.
❷ Finely chop the parsley and onion, and combine in a bowl with the salmon and egg yolk.
❸ Season with salt and pepper. Add the cognac, then allow to sit for approx. 30 minutes.
❹ Shape the tartare on a plate before serving.

TOP TIP

Make sure the salmon you buy is sashimi quality – a quality seal indicating the requisite product grade for preparation of raw fish dishes such as sushi. Stricter criteria apply when raw ingredients are to be used.

TABOULÉ SALAD

with tomatoes, mint and lemon

PREPARATION

❶ Bring 100 ml (3½ fl oz/scant ½ cup) water to the boil in a saucepan, then turn the heat down, add the burghul and leave to swell for 10 minutes. The burghul will absorb all the water. Tip into a large bowl and leave to cool.

❷ Dice the tomatoes and slice the spring onions (scallions) into thin rings. Finely chop the parsley and mint, then mix all the fresh ingredients with the bulgur. Add the olive oil.

❸ Finally, season the salad with the lemon juice, salt and pepper.

4

FOR 4 PEOPLE

50 g (1¾ oz/¼ cup) burghul
400 g (14 oz) firm tomatoes
4 spring onions (scallions)
2 bunches of parsley
1 bunch of mint
5 tbsp olive oil
1½ lemons
salt & pepper

PARIS
Syndrome

The German couple moved into their apartment in a Paris suburb proud and happy, and introduced themselves to their French neighbours. The reaction of the latter was a surprise: first sympathy, then blatant disbelief that these Germans had actually come to Paris of their own free will. The city is admittedly interesting, but: *la pollution, le trafic, le stress* ... It's true – seen up close, the dream described in the tourist publicity has its flip side: Paris is a modern city – sometimes noisy and dirty, often hectic and overcrowded, full of stark contrasts between rich and poor. If you've been expecting Chanel fragrances to the accompaniment of gentle accordion music, then an overcrowded Métro or drug-addicted prostitutes at the station may come as quite a shock. Many exhausted tourists stay in their holiday apartment on their second or third day, and even there they don't get any peace and quiet, as some apartments are very thin-walled and all sorts of smells from the courtyards penetrate through the windows.

Travellers from Japan and, increasingly, Chinese visitors are even more shocked than European tourists at the mismatch between dream and reality. They arrive in the city with images in their head from the film Amélie or the Louis Vuitton catalogue, and on top of that have to overcome the general culture shock experienced by those coming to Europe from the Far East.

Every year the Paris hospitals register patients in a distraught state as a result of this shock, and the malaise has been dubbed *Paris Syndrome*. Parisians themselves are often unaware of the extent to which their city is romanticised in advertising abroad. They've nicknamed Paris *Paname* (Panama), referencing an investment swindle that promised people fabulous returns overseas and ultimately cheated them out of their money – Paris, too, means promises and disappointment.

Despite all this Parisians love their city – in their own way. *Amoureux de Paname* (Paris Lovers) is the title of a song from the 70s, which is about asphalt, concrete and air pollution. As with every big city, e.g. New York and Berlin, you sometimes have to put up with wildness, ugliness and noise in order to discover the golden heart of the city.

PARIS SYNDROME AND THE BISTROS You can also be hit by *Paris Syndrome* when going out for a meal. You can eat very well in Paris, but anyone expecting the food to be good everywhere will be disappointed: you'll sometimes be served a floppy croque monsieur at a bar, heated-up frozen food at a restaurant or a mediocre café au lait for €10 at a fancy establishment – this can happen in Paris.

But what you can do is to prepare well. If you wearily rush into the first bistro you come across as soon as you're hungry, there's a good chance you'll be disappointed. A better idea is to seek out a few good addresses for your target area beforehand. And the time of day is important, because many restaurants and bistros don't serve hot food in the afternoon. If you want to eat at 3pm the choice of outlets is restricted, and you'll have to compromise.

NB: at lunchtime on weekdays many restaurants offer a cheaper menu *(Formule)* or a dish of the day *(Plat du jour)*. With a little luck this will mean ingredients fresh from the market at a good price. Smaller, traditional bistros won't always have vegetarian or vegan dishes on their menu, but it's worth asking. Sometimes the answer will be 'Chef will sort something out for you,' and the result will be surprisingly delicious.

Many Paris restaurants work on the basis of two sittings per evening. Some people arrive at 8pm – the normal time for an evening meal – and others at 10pm, after the theatre or cinema, leaving enough time for a relaxing meal. But those wishing to round the evening off with a few glasses of wine usually go on to a bar. You should expect the bill to come quickly, with the unvoiced expectation that you'll make way for the next guests.

It's often said that the French 'refuse' to speak other languages, but they would counter that they're 'embarrassed' about their poor language skills. This embarrassment can come over as slight arrogance. If you can, you should try to break the ice with a few words of French, even if you stress words wrongly and your grammar is poor.

EVENING MEAL
Le Plats

Blanquette de Veau

FRENCH VEAL STEW

Slow and very long cooking here is key.
The crème fraîche gives the blanquette a perfect creamy consistency. Serve
with rice or potatoes, or just a baguette, French-style.

4

FOR 4 PEOPLE

1 kg (2 lb 4 oz) veal
2 large carrots
2 leeks
200 g (7 oz) mushrooms
1 onion
1 stick of celery
3 tbsp butter
1 bay leaf
1 sprig of thyme
30 g (1 oz) flour
200 ml (7 fl oz/scant 1 cup)
crème fraîche
1 egg yolk
juice of 1 lemon
2 stems of parsley
salt & pepper

PREPARATION

❶ Cut the veal into bite-sized pieces.
❷ Slice the carrots and leeks. Halve or quarter the mushrooms, depending on size. Finely dice the onion and celery.
❸ Melt 1 tablespoon butter in a large ovenproof pan and briefly sauté the meat and vegetables together with the bay leaf and thyme, plus a little salt and pepper.
❹ Pour enough water to cover the meat and vegetables, and bring to the boil. Skim away any foam from the surface until the stock is clear.
❺ Simmer the stew for approx. 2½ hours.
❻ Melt the remaining butter in a saucepan and stir in the flour. Gradually add the stock to the roux, then briefly bring to the boil. Whisk the sauce until creamy. Now add the meat and vegetables.
❼ Mix the crème fraîche, egg yolk, lemon juice, salt and pepper in a bowl, and add to the stew.
❽ Finely chop the parsley, and garnish the *blanquette de veau* with it before serving.

BŒUF BOURGUIGNON

This dish needs a bit of planning in advance, as the beef needs to be marinated overnight. This step of letting the meat sit overnight in a marinade of red wine, bay leaf, herbes de Provence, garlic and pepper makes for a real depth of flavour in the finished stew. This also tastes even better the next day.

4

FOR 4 PEOPLE

1 kg (2 lb 4 oz) beef shank
2 large onions
2 carrots
1 clove of garlic
2 bay leaves
2 sprigs of thyme
1 sprig of rosemary
1 bunch of parsley
1 bottle (750 ml/25 fl oz/3 cups) of
red wine (preferably Burgundy)
100 g (3½ oz) bacon
1 tablespoon flour
salt & pepper

PREPARATION

❶ Cut the beef into large pieces, cut the onions into rings and slice the carrots.
❷ Steep the meat in the red wine overnight, together with the vegetables, the clove of garlic and the herbs.
❸ Remove the beef from the wine mixture, and drain on kitchen paper. Keep the vegetable and wine marinade aside. Dice the bacon and fry in a large saucepan. Add the beef to the pan, and brown it all over.
❹ Remove the beef from the pan, cover and leave to one side. Now remove the onion from the reserved marinade and gently braise in the pan.
❺ Return the beef to the pan. Sprinkle with the flour and cook for a few minutes, stirring to stop it burning.
❻ Now add the remaining vegetables along with their wine marinade, and season with salt and pepper.
❼ Simmer for 3 hours over a low heat.
❽ Finely chop the parsley, and sprinkle over the bœuf bourguignon before serving.

TOP TIP
When choosing a red wine simply trust your palette, and ideally use one you like drinking.

Ratatouille

2

FOR 2 PEOPLE

1 aubergine (eggplant)
350 g (12 oz) tomatoes
1 onion
1 clove of garlic
olive oil
1 courgette (zucchini)
½ red (bell) pepper
½ green pepper
2 tbsp olive oil
1 sprig of thyme
1 sprig of rosemary
salt & pepper

PREPARATION

❶ Cut the aubergine (eggplant) into small cubes, sprinkle with a little salt and leave to sit for 10 minutes.

❷ Peel and core the tomatoes. To do so, scald them with hot water so the skin can be pulled off more easily. Then cut them up small.

❸ Cut the onion into cubes and chop the garlic.

❹ Slice the courgette (zucchini) and (bell) peppers into thin strips.

❺ In a large saucepan sauté the onion and garlic in a little olive oil.

❻ Pat the aubergine (eggplant) dry, add to the pan and fry until golden brown. Then add the (bell) peppers. Season with the thyme, rosemary, salt and pepper, and cook over a low heat for 20 minutes.

❼ After 20 minutes stir in the tomatoes and sliced courgette.

❽ Bring to the boil. If necessary, add a little water. Don't simmer the vegetables for too long, to make sure they stay al dente.

❾ Before serving, season to taste with salt and pepper and remove the herbs.

TOP TIP

On hot summer days Ratatouille can also be served cold.

COQ AU VIN

Roosters are traditionally used for this recipe in France, but you can use either corn-fed chicken, or chicken thighs. However, the taste is more intense if you use a whole rooster or chicken. Equally important is a good red wine, ideally a Bordeaux.

4

FOR 4 PEOPLE

1 rooster or chicken
750 ml (75 fl oz/3 cups) red wine
2 sprigs of thyme
3 bay leaves
4 juniper berries
1 clove
2 tbsp butter
500 ml (17 fl oz/generous 2 cups) water
½ bunch of parsley
2 onions
3 cloves of garlic
200 g (7 oz) bacon
1 small glass of cognac
300 ml beef stock
300 g (10½ oz) carrots
300 g (10½ oz) mushrooms
12 baby onions
2 small pieces of dark chocolate
salt & pepper

❶ Divide the bird into large pieces the evening before, and separate off the breast pieces and the thighs. Set the carcass to one side for the stock.

❷ Prepare the marinade: put the red wine, 1 sprig of thyme, 2 bay leaves, the juniper berries and the clove into a bowl. Lay the poultry pieces in it, and marinate in the fridge overnight.

❸ For the stock, brown the remaining poultry pieces in a saucepan with 1 tablespoon of butter. Then cover with water, and add a bouquet of herbs comprising a bay leaf, a sprig of thyme and the parsley. Reduce the stock to half, then pass it through a sieve and keep refrigerated.

❹ The next day, remove the poultry pieces from the marinade and dry off on kitchen paper. Keep the marinade aside.

❺ Cut the onions into rings and finely chop the garlic.

❻ In a large saucepan add the remaining butter and brown the bacon, then put to one side. Using the same fat, brown the poultry pieces and likewise put to one side.

❼ Brown the onions together with the garlic. Add the poultry to the pan and immediately deglaze with cognac. Then add the marinade and the stock, and simmer together for 1¾ hours.

❽ Preheat the oven to 180°C (400°F). Remove the poultry pieces from the pan, and transfer to a casserole dish with a little sauce and cook for 45 minutes.

❾ Meanwhile chop the carrots and mushrooms, and add to the remaining sauce in the pan together with the baby onions. Add the beef stock and the chocolate. Bring to the boil over a medium heat, and simmer until thickened.

❿ Season the sauce with salt and pepper.

⓫ Remove the poultry from the oven and return it to the pan with the vegetables.

MOULES FRITES
MUSSELS WITH FRENCH FRIES

2

INGREDIENTS

1 to 1.5 kg (2 lb 4 oz–3 lb 5 oz)
mussels
1 clove of garlic
1 shallot
1 leek
20 g (¾ oz) butter
500 ml (17 fl oz/generous 2 cups)
white wine (e.g. Sauvignon Blanc)
½ bunch of parsley
salt & pepper

FOR THE FRENCH FRIES

4 large potatoes (waxy)
4 tbsp vegetable oil
½ tsp paprika
1 tsp sea salt

PREPARATION

❶ For the fries, peel the potatoes and cut into long sticks. Then put into a bowl of water, to release some of the starch from them.

❷ Preheat the oven to 180°C fan (400°F). Line a baking sheet with parchment paper.

❸ Pat the potatoes dry with kitchen paper, and mix with the vegetable oil, paprika and salt in a bowl. Lay on the prepared baking sheet and bake for 50 minutes, until they're golden brown and crispy.

❹ Wash the mussels thoroughly. Remove any open or damaged mussels and dispose of them.

❺ Finely chop the garlic and shallot. Cut the leek into rings.

❻ Melt the butter in a saucepan, add the garlic, shallot and leek and sauté until softened.

❼ Deglaze with the white wine, season with salt and pepper and bring it all to the boil.

❽ Add the mussels and boil for 5 to 7 minutes with the lid on.

❾ Chop the parsley and sprinkle over the top before serving.

TOP TIP

If you have one, the French fries should ideally be cooked in a deep-fat fryer. This will make them even crunchier.

GRATIN DAUPHINOIS

For an excellent gratin dauphinois the potatoes must be preboiled, then cooked in the oven at a moderate heat. A gratin is traditionally made without cheese and is served with meat dishes.

4

FOR 4 PEOPLE

1 kg (2 lb 4 oz) potatoes
1 clove of garlic
3 tbsp butter
1 litre (34 fl oz/4¼ cups) milk
250 ml (8 fl oz) crème fraiche
grated nutmeg
salt & pepper

PREPARATION

❶ Peel the potatoes and put in cold water, to release some of the starch from them.
❷ Halve the garlic, grease a casserole dish with 1 tablespoon butter, rub with the garlic halves, then finely chop them.
❸ Dry the potatoes with kitchen paper and cut into thin slices. Season the sliced potato with salt and pepper.
❹ Preheat the oven to 190°C fan (400°F).
❺ Mix the milk and crème frâiche in a saucepan, then add the sliced potatoes. Season with nutmeg.
❻ Briefly bring to the boil, and simmer for approx. 10 minutes over a low heat, making sure the potatoes remain covered and the milk (add a little more milk if needed) doesn't burn.
❼ Put the potatoes and milk mixture into a casserole dish. Once again, ensure the potatoes remain covered. Dot the remaining butter on top.
❽ Before the dish goes into the oven, reduce the temperature to 150°C fan (350°F). Bake the gratin for 45 minutes, until the potatoes are soft and the top is golden brown.

FILET DE BŒUF
WITH BÉARNAISE SAUCE

2

INGREDIENTS

300 g (1 lb 2 oz) beef tenderloin
coarsely ground sea salt &
peppercorns
50 g (1¾ oz) butter

BÉARNAISE SAUCE

1 shallot
250 g (9 oz) butter
½ tbsp white-wine vinegar
½ tbsp white wine
3 egg yolks
½ tbsp lemon juice
1 stem of tarragon
salt & pepper

PREPARATION

❶ Preheat the oven to 150°C fan (350°F).
Coarsely grind the sea salt and the peppercorns
using a pestle and mortar. Rub the beef with the
salt and pepper mixture.
❷ Heat a pan over a high heat. Add the butter and
sear the beef in the pan all over. Then transfer to
an ovenproof dish or casserole, and put in the
oven for 20 to 30 minutes.
❸ Meanwhile, prepare the béarnaise sauce. Finely
chop the shallot. Melt the butter in a saucepan
(see Tip). In another saucepan, bring the vinegar,
white wine and shallot to the boil, and reduce by
about half.
❹ Remove the white-wine stock from the heat,
briefly cool, and carefully – to avoid curdling – fold
in the egg yolks, until a creamy consistency is
achieved.
❺ Then add the melted butter, stirring constantly,
and season with the salt, pepper and lemon juice.
❻ Remove the tarragon leaves and shoot tips
from the stem, finely chop and add to the
béarnaise sauce.
❼ Take the beef out of the oven, wrap in kitchen
foil and rest for 15 minutes. Slice up before
serving with the béarnaise sauce.

TIPS

To prevent the butter burning, add a dash
of vegetable oil to the pan.

This dish goes particularly well with
the Gratin Dauphinois (page 95).

BISTROS

ET CETERA

BOUILLONS The word bistro found its way into the English language quite some time ago, likewise bouillon. Since the end of the 19th century, however, in Paris a bouillon has been the name not only for a stock but also for a simple restaurant where you can get a single lunch dish at a reasonable price. Some modern bouillons are now invoking this tradition. They offer a nostalgic ambience and a simple menu comprising traditional French dishes at reasonable prices. Just search for 'Bouillon Paris' on Google Maps, then locate one near to you!

BISTROTS DU QUARTIER In the famous crime novels about the Parisian DCI Maigret the lunchtime restaurant visits are a fixed point of reference. They help him immerse himself in the atmosphere of the quarter. To this very day bistros and small restaurants are far more part of Parisians' everyday life than is the case in Britain. Lunch breaks are normally much more generous than they are here, so as to allow time for a good meal. By law, companies must either provide their employees with a canteen or offer them *chèques-restaurants* (restaurant luncheon vouchers), so at lunchtime many bistros have regular customers from their part of the city.
These bistros offer their guests honest French home cooking, not delicacies or experiments, and the ambience may also be decidedly unromantic. We've chosen a few examples from the less fashionable districts in the east of the city, where you'll feel as if you're in DCI Maigret's Paris.

CREATIVE CUISINE Tradition isn't everything, not even in Paris. Alongside the traditional bistros there are of course also chefs who try out new things, have light and airy furnishings, combine unusual ingredients, buy organic produce, do gluten-free or vegan dishes … Here we've just put together a few examples from the diverse offering.

100

THREE SPECIAL SMALL MUSEUMS

MUSÉE MARMOTTAN A trip to Paris usually includes a museum or gallery visit. If you love the impressionists you'll doubtless first think of the Musée d'Orsay. It's really huge, and full of impressive treasures. Actually there's not usually enough time to take everything in properly, and there are long queues to get in. You really need to allow a whole day for it.
The Musée Marmottan, on the other hand, is a lovely little museum housed in a 19th-century mansion that has been kept in its original state. The collection includes numerous impressionist masterpieces, e.g. Monet's Water Lilies, but it's not a huge museum with hordes of visitors, thus an afternoon will suffice.

MUSÉE DES ARTS ET METIERS Situated near the Canal Saint Martin, this isn't obligatory for everyone, like the Louvre is, but it's a real find for nostalgic techno-freaks and steampunkers. There are picturesque double-deckers hanging in a deconsecrated church, charming 18th-century puppets moving as if by magic and shining brass steam engines. As well as its picturesque and enchanting side, the museum time and again offers explanations and models for experimentation and participation.

MUSÉE RODIN This wonderful little museum on the Left Bank of the Seine doesn't overwhelm you with super-abundance. As the name indicates it's dedicated to the artist and sculptor Auguste Rodin, and displays not only his works but also items from its collection of antiquities. A separate hall is dedicated to his artistic partner and lover Camille Claudel. The Musée Rodin is housed in an 18th-century mansion, and the artworks are exhibited in the building and its park. It's worth making a detour to the museum café in the park.

MUSÉE MARMOTTAN
2, Rue Louis-Boilly,
16th arrondissement
metro station La Muette

MUSÉE DES ARTS
ET METIERS
60 Rue de Reaumur,
3rd arrondissement
metro station Arts et Métiers

MUSÉE RODIN
77, Rue de Varenne,
7. arrondissement

DESSERTS
or
CHEESE

105

THE PERFECT CHEESE BOARD

CHEESE OR DESSERT? One often hears this in French restaurants. As a saying it means you can't have everything – you have to decide. But with a big menu you're of course offered *fromage et dessert*!

A cheese course before the dessert is a staple part of the menu, usually in the form of a cheese board from which each guest chooses something. Bread – usually baguettes – will already be on the table.

Such a cheese board normally includes the following:

4 or 5 types of cheese, which are as varied as possible. Maybe a goat's cheese, as a roll or 'thaler', a hard cheese like Morbier, Ossau-Iraty or Comté, a blue cheese such as Roquefort or Saint Agur, a cheese in the style of a Chaumes or Langres, something from Germany, e.g. L'Amour Rouge d'Antoine, and a Brie, Camembert etc.

In Paris a *Brie de Meaux* is often served, as Meaux is fairly nearby. Do try it – it's fresher and creamier than many exported Bries!

A cheese board is also a great opportunity to serve Chaumes or Munster. They're cheeses you'd rarely buy for yourself on account of their strong smell.

Figs and grapes are suitable as fresh-tasting accompaniments to cheese – and mustard, fig mustard and quince paste are also good complements.

Wines to go with cheese should be on the fresh and sweet side, ideally white wines, e.g. Sauvignon Blanc and Gewürztraminer, or sweet Muscat wines such as Muscat de Rivesaltes and Muscat de Beaumes de Venise.

TOP TIPS

Take the cheese out of the fridge about half an hour before serving, so the aroma can develop, and put each type on a wooden board with a knife.

Round cheeses should be cut like pies, to minimise the cut edges!

CHARLOTTE
aux Fraises

When it is strawberry season this is on every menu – it tastes fruity and fresh, plus it looks elegant. A charlotte is lighter than you think but just needs a little planning, as it should be prepared the evening before.

FOR 4 PEOPLE

400 g (14 oz) strawberries
400 ml (14 fl oz/generous 1½ cups)
whipping cream
60 g (2 oz) sugar
250 g (9 oz) mascarpone
grated zest of 1 lime
10 mint leaves
juice of ⅓ lime
butter for greasing
30 sponge fingers

A charlotte cake tin (pan) or small
saucepan (approx. 18 cm/7 in wide
and at least 8 cm/3¼ in high)

PREPARATION

❶ First put 6 to 8 large strawberries to one side.
❷ In a bowl, beat the whipping cream with 50 g (1¾ oz) sugar until stiff. In a second bowl, mix the mascarpone until creamy, and fold into the whipped cream together with the lime zest. Spoon into a piping bag and leave to cool.
❸ Finely chop 8 mint leaves. Cut the strawberries into small cubes. Mix with the lime juice, remaining sugar and the mint. Put to one side, so the strawberries can release some juice.
❹ Grease the charlotte cake tin (pan) with a little butter. Now arrange the sponge fingers around the edge, sugared side outwards, and cover the base of the pan with them.
❺ Scoop off the juice of the strawberries, and spread on the sponge fingers using a brush.
❻ Now spread a third of the mascarpone cream mixture on the base using the piping bag, then cover with half of the strawberries. Place a further 3 to 4 sponge fingers on top (if necessary cut to size, so they fit). Finally spread with another third of the cream mixture, then top with the remaining strawberries and finish with the rest of the cream mixture.
❼ Leave in the fridge overnight.
❽ The next day, carefully turn out. Slice the strawberries you put to one side, and coat the charlotte with them in a fan shape.

Crème Brûlée

The simplest way to achieve the crème brûlée's delicious, crispy caramel crust is to cool the crème well, then caramelise the sprinkled sugar using a small blowtorch. If you don't have a blowtorch, you can use your oven to caramelise the sugar or place under the grill, with the temperature set to maximum ... Keep an eye on it, as the caramel can burn easily via these methods.

6

FOR 6 PEOPLE

1½ vanilla pods
2 whole eggs
8 egg yolks
160 g (5½ oz/¾ cup) sugar
800 ml (27 fl oz) cream
75 g (2½ oz) brown sugar

PREPARATION

❶ Preheat the oven to 130°C fan (300°F).
❷ Split the vanilla pods lengthwise, and scrape the vanilla seeds into a bowl. Add the eggs, egg yolks and sugar, and stir.
❸ In another bowl, beat the cream until stiff, and carefully fold into the egg mixture.
❹ Pour the crème into 6 ovenproof ramekins, place in a deep baking tray, pour in a little water and bake in the oven for 40 minutes.
❺ Remove and cool the crème in the ramekins – overnight, if possible.
❻ Before serving the crème brûlée, generously sprinkle with brown sugar and caramelise with a small blow torch (or see introduction).

Crêpes Suzette

The idea of flambéing crêpes arose back at the end of the 19th century. Not only do the flames look spectacular – they also ensure that the alcohol is almost completely burnt off and the sugar is caramelised, and make for a particularly good blending of the aromas.

2

FOR 2 PEOPLE

70 g (2½ oz) flour
1 egg
1 pinch of salt
50 g (1¾ oz) sugar
150 ml (5 fl oz/scant ⅔ cup) milk
70 g soft butter, plus extra
for frying
grated zest of 1 orange
20 g (¾ oz) icing (powdered) sugar
4 tbsp orange liqueur

TOP TIP
When flambéing, put everything that might catch fire out of reach (and tie your hair up!).

PREPARATION

❶ Blend the flour, eggs and salt in a bowl. Add the sugar and 50 ml (1¾ fl oz/3½ tablespoons) milk, and whisk to form a smooth batter.

❷ Melt 50 g (1¾ oz) butter in a saucepan. Gradually add the remaining milk to the batter, the melted butter and half the grated orange zest. Let it rest in the fridge for at least 2 hours.

❸ One by one, fry the crêpes with a little butter in a pan, and stack on a plate. It's best to cover them, so they stay warm and don't dry out.

❹ For the orange crème, mix the icing (powdered) sugar, the remaining grated orange zest and 20 g (¾ oz) soft butter in a bowl.

❺ Spread some orange crème on each crêpe and fold to form a triangle.

❻ Ten minutes before serving the crêpes, briefly warm them up in an oven heated to 150°C fan (350°F).

❼ One by one, sprinkle the crêpes with icing (powdered) sugar in a pan, and heat them up. In a small, deep pan, or a small saucepan, heat the liqueur to approx. 40°C (100°F). Light the liqueur and pour the hot, still flaming liqueur over the crêpes.

Faisselle
COULIS DE FRAISE

A coulis is a puréed fruit sauce. Slightly sweetened, it tastes good with ice cream, yoghurt and cakes. In the hot summer months raspberries, apricots and ripe peaches are also great seasonal substitutes.

FOR 2 PEOPLE

1 faisselle (or 250 g/9 oz quark)
150 g (5½ oz) strawberries
1 tbsp sugar
juice of ½ lemon

PREPARATION

❶ Drain the faisselle or quark in a sieve lined with muslin cloth.
❷ Put 4 strawberries to one side for the decoration. Chop the remaining strawberries into small pieces.
❸ Purée the chopped strawberries together with the sugar and lemon juice, and – if you want to get rid of the little pips in the strawberry purée – pass through a fine sieve.
❹ Stir the faisselle or quark until creamy, and spoon into small bowls or glasses. Pour the strawberry purée on top.
❺ Decorate with the reserved strawberries and leave to cool for approx. 1 hour.

TOP TIP
You might find faisselle, a French cheese made of raw milk, in a cheese shop, but if you use a supermarket quark this dish will taste (nearly) as good as the original. Twaróg tastes quite similar to faisselle, and is available from Polish and Russian supermarkets.

FONDANT
au Chocolat

In English this cake is popularly known as 'death by chocolate'. It's sinfully chocolatey and unbeatably tasty – whether on its own, with cream or a scoop of vanilla ice cream.

6

FOR ONE 26 CM (10¼ IN) ROUND TIN OR 6 SMALL MOULDS

200 g (7 oz) dark chocolate
200 g (7 oz) butter
130 g (4½ oz) icing (powdered) sugar
25 g (¾ oz) flour
4 eggs
a little butter for greasing

PREPARATION

❶ Preheat the oven to 150°C fan (350°F).
❷ Cut the chocolate up into small pieces, and melt in a bain-marie. Cut the butter into small pieces and stir into the melted chocolate until they are both melted and have formed a creamy mixture.
❸ Remove the chocolate mixture from the heat and gradually add the sugar, flour and eggs. The batter should be smooth and workable.
❹ Grease the tin or moulds with a little butter, then dust with flour, so the cake(s) can be turned out more easily after baking. Pour the batter into the tin or moulds, and place in the preheated oven.
❺ Depending on the size of the tin/moulds, the fondant baking time will vary. The small moulds will need approx. 15 to 20 minutes, whilst a large baking tin will need approx. 20 to 30 minutes. Testing with a skewer is a good idea, as the centre of the fondant au chocolat should be runny.
❻ Turn the still-warm fondant(s) au chocolat out of the tin/moulds, and sprinkle with the icing (powdered) sugar.

Madeleines
WITH HONEY

PREPARATION

❶ Melt the butter in a saucepan, and allow to cool.
❷ Mix the flour with the baking powder in a bowl.
Beat the egg with the sugar and honey in another
bowl, and slowly add the flour mixture.
❸ Add the ground almonds, lemon juice and lemon
zest, mix, and right at the end stir in the melted
butter.
❹ Rest the mixture in the fridge for at least
20 minutes, and meanwhile preheat the oven
to 180°C fan (400°F).
❺ Remove the mixture from the fridge, and once
again beat it.
❻ Pour in the mixture into the madeleine tray until
each mould of the madeleine tray is two-thirds
full, and bake for 12 minutes.
❼ Let the madeleines cool in the baking tray,
as this will help them come out more easily.

**FOR APPROX.
12 MADELEINES**

40 g (1½ oz) butter
40 g (1½ oz) flour
½ tsp baking powder
1 egg
45 g (1½ oz) sugar
1 tsp honey
20 g (¾ oz) ground almonds
1 tbsp lemon juice
1 tsp grated lemon zest

madeleine tray

Mousse
au Chocolat

6

FOR 6 PEOPLE

200 g (7 oz) dark chocolate
5 eggs
150 ml (5 fl oz/scant ⅔ cup)
whipping cream
3 tbsp sugar

PREPARATION

❶ Melt the chocolate in a bain-marie. Allow to cool.
❷ Separate the eggs. Beat the whipping cream and the egg whites separately until stiff.
❸ Mix the egg yolks with the sugar until creamy, then slowly add the melted chocolate. Carefully fold in the whipped cream.
❹ Fold the egg whites into the mousse, a little at a time, to create a smooth mixture.
❺ Pour the finished mousse au chocolat into a bowl, and leave to cool for at least 3 to 4 hours.

TARTE RUSTIQUE À LA
RHUBARBE

FOR ONE 26 CM (10¼ IN) TART FOR 12 PEOPLE

INGREDIENTS

730 g (1 lb 10 oz) rhubarb
150 g (5½ oz) raw sugar
80 g (2¾ oz) water
a pinch of salt
250 g (9 oz) flour
200 g (7 oz) butter
100 g (3½ oz) ground almonds
2 eggs, beaten

TOP TIP

Ground hazelnuts work very well
in this tart instead of ground
almonds.

PREPARATION

❶ Peel the rhubarb, and cut into parallelogram-shaped pieces, as in the photo. Place in a bowl and sprinkle with 50g (1¾ oz) sugar.
❷ Preheat the oven to 170°C.
❸ Add a pinch of salt to the water.
❹ Put the flour into a bowl, add 100g (3½ oz) butter and rub this into the flour.
❺ Add the salted water and knead the mixture to form a smooth dough. Shape into a ball, and let it rest in a cool place for 30 minutes.
❻ On a dusted surface, roll the dough out to form a round. Then lay on a baking sheet lined with parchment paper.
❼ For the almond crème, beat 100 g (3½ oz) softened butter and 100 g (3½ oz) raw sugar to form a creamy mixture. Add the ground almonds and the beaten eggs to the butter/sugar mixture, and mix together well.
❽ Prick the pastry base with a fork at regular intervals, spread with the almond crème and smooth it, leaving an approx. 2 cm (¾ in) edge free border. Arrange the rhubarb pieces on the pastry, and fold the edge over.
❾ Put the tart in the oven and bake for 45 to 50 minutes.

TARTE AU CITRON
Meringuée

**This quick, simple tart is a classic dessert that is very popular.
It tastes fresh, and is not too sweet.**

8

**FOR SEVERAL SMALL TARTES
AU CITRON OR ONE LARGE TART
(26 CM/10¼ IN)**

200 ml (7 fl oz/scant 1 cup) lemon
juice (approx. 3 to 4 lemons)
310 g (11 oz) sugar
180 g (6½ oz) butter
1 tbsp cornflour (cornstarch)
3 eggs
200 g (7 oz/1⅔ cups) flour
1 pinch of salt
½ glass of cold water
2 egg whites
1 tbsp vanilla sugar

PREPARATION

❶ For the crème, pour the lemon juice into a saucepan and slowly heat together with 150 g (5½ oz) sugar and 80 g (2¾ oz) butter, until everything has combined to make a smooth liquid. Carefully add the cornflour (cornstarch) and stir.

❷ Crack the eggs into a bowl and beat. Gradually add the lemon mixture to the eggs, and mix everything together. Then return it all to the saucepan, and heat the crème until it thickens, whilst constantly stirring.

❸ Spoon the finished crème into jars or a bowl, and leave to cool. It will keep for several days like this.

❹ Preheat the oven to 180°C fan (350°F).

❺ For the shortcrust pastry knead the flour together with 100 g (3½ oz) butter, then stir in 20 g (¾ oz) sugar and the water to form a smooth dough. Shape the dough into a ball, then let it rest in the fridge for 30 minutes.

❻ Roll the dough out thinly, and lay in the tin or moulds. Prick with a fork at regular intervals, line with parchment paper, weigh down with dried pulses and blind bake for 10 minutes.

❼ Remove from the oven and allow to cool. Spread the finished crème in the pastry shell.

❽ Beat the two egg whites together with 140 g (5 oz) sugar and the vanilla sugar until stiff. Fill the egg-white mixture into a piping bag and squeeze out little dabs or florets onto the lemon tart(s). Using a blowtorch, brown and caramelise the egg-white florets.

IMAGE CREDITS

First published in the German in 2022 under the title: Zu Tish in Paris
© 2022 Jan Thorbecke Verlag, Verlagsgruppe Patmos in der
Schabenverlag AG, Ostfildern

This English edition publish in 2024 by Hardie Grant Books,
an imprint of Hardie Grant Publishing

Hardie Grant Books (London)
5th & 6th Floors
52–54 Southwark Street
London SE1 1UN

Hardie Grant Books (Melbourne)
Building 1, 658 Church Street
Richmond, Victoria 3121

hardiegrantbooks.com

British Library Cataloguing-in-Publication Data. A catalogue record
this book is available from the British Library.

At the Table in Paris
ISBN: 978-1-78488-691-2

10 9 8 7 6 5 4 3 2 1

Publishing Director: Kajal Mistry
Commissioning Editor: Kate Burkett
Senior Editor: Eila Purvis
Translator: William Sleath
Typesettor: David Meikle
Proofreader: Kate Wanwimolruk
Production Controller: Sabeena Atchia

Colour reproduction by p2d
Printed and bound in China by Leo Paper Products Ltd.